Descendants

OF

JAMES ROYAL BADGETT

Descendants of James Royal Badgett

Generation 1

1.   **JAMES ROYAL[1] BADGETT** was born on 04 Apr 1834 in North Carolina. He died on 07 Mar 1908 in Texas. He married (1) **MARY BELLE WAKEFIELD**, daughter of John Wakefield and Sitha Ann Fleet on 14 Sep 1871 in Warren County, Kentucky. She was born on 10 Aug 1844 in Warren County, Kentucky. She died on 16 Sep 1885 in Bells, Texas. He married (2) **ANNA M. WAKEFIELD**, daughter of John Wakefield and Sitha Ann Fleet on 22 Dec 1864 in Bowling Green, Warren County, Kentucky. She was born about 1842 in Kentucky. She died between 10 Jun 1870-14 Sep 1871.

More About James Royal Badgett:
Burial: Old Bells North Cemetery, Bells, Texas
Occupation: 1850 in Tar River District, Granville County, North Carolina; Farmer
Occupation: 1870 in Bowling Green, Warren County, Kentucky; Stock Trader
Occupation: 1880 in Rich Pond, Warren County, Kentucky; Farmer
Occupation: 05 Apr 1887 in Bells, Texas; Elected as Alderman
Occupation: 1894 in Hall County, Texas; Justice of the Peace
Occupation: 1896 in Hall County, Texas; Justice of the Peace
Occupation: Bet. 1898-1900; County Treasurer, Hall County, Texas

More About Mary Belle Wakefield:
b: 10 Aug 1844
Burial: Old Bells North Cemetery, Bells, Texas
Living In: 1870 Living in the household of her brother in law, James Royal Badgett, and sister, Anna, in Bowling Green, Kentucky.

James Royal Badgett and Mary Belle Wakefield had the following children:

2.   i. ANNIE LEE[2] BADGETT was born on 04 Aug 1872 in Bowling Green, Kentucky. She died on 01 Jan 1956 in Sherman, Texas. She married Henry William Witcher, son of James Coleman Witcher and Mildred Fannie Gilbert on 18 Oct 1888 in Sherman, Texas. He was born on 28 Sep 1868 in Missouri. He died on 02 Dec 1941 in Sherman, Grayson County, Texas.

ii.   JOHN W. BADGETT was born about 1876 in Kentucky.

3.   iii. SAMUEL E. BADGETT was born on 19 Jun 1878 in Warren County, Kentucky. He died on 31 Aug 1909 in Texas. He married MARY MAXEY BELOTE. She was born on 07 Oct 1880 in Grayson County, Texas. She died on 22 May 1963 in Sherman, Texas.

4.   iv. CLAUDE RAY BADGETT was born on 27 Jan 1881 in Kentuckytown, Grayson County, Texas. He died on 18 Apr 1960 in Plainview, Texas. He married Annie Bell Bowie, daughter of Alexander Bowie and Barbara Patterson Bell on 16 Apr 1902 in Coalgate, Choctaw Nation, Indian Territory (Present Day Oklahoma). She was born on 11 Mar 1886 in Krebs, Indian Territory (Present Day Oklahoma). She died on 31 Jan 1978 in Amarillo, Potter County, Texas.

James Royal Badgett and Anna M. Wakefield had the following child: v.
BLANCHE BADGETT was born in 1866 in Kentucky.

Generation 2

2.   **ANNIE LEE[2] BADGETT** (James Royal[1]) was born on 04 Aug 1872 in Bowling Green, Kentucky. She died on 01 Jan 1956 in Sherman, Texas. She married Henry William Witcher, son of James Coleman Witcher and Mildred Fannie Gilbert on 18 Oct 1888 in Sherman, Texas. He was born on 28 Sep 1868 in Missouri. He died on 02 Dec 1941 in Sherman, Grayson County, Texas.

More About Annie Lee Badgett:
Burial: 03 Jan 1956 in Old Bells North Cemetery, Bells, Texas
Cause Of Death: Coronary Thrombosis

More About Henry William Witcher:
Burial: 04 Dec 1941 in Old Bells North Cemetery, Bells, Texas
Cause Of Death: Coronary Thrombosis
Living In: 1930 Sherman, Grayson County, Texas
Living In: 1940 Sherman, Grayson County, Texas
Occupation: 1900 in Bells, Grayson County, Texas; Dealer in Drugs
Occupation: 1910 in Bells, Grayson County, Texas; Owner of "City Drug Store"
Occupation: 1920 in Bells, Grayson County, Texas; Real Estate Broker
Occupation: Banker

Henry William Witcher and Annie Lee Badgett had the following children:

5.   i. OPAL[3] WITCHER was born in May 1893 in Texas. She died in 1973 in Grayson County, Texas. She married CHARLES W. ANDERSON.

6.   ii. FANNIE BELL WITCHER was born on 27 Jan 1897 in Bells, Texas. She died in Oct 1962 in Hobart, Oklahoma. She married William Preston Dugan, son of William Preston Dugan and Lydia Vernon Jones in 1914 in Bells, Texas. He was born on 11 Dec 1893 in Bells, Texas. He died in 1956 in Hobart, Oklahoma.

    iii. EMMA LEE WITCHER was born on 19 Aug 1901 in Bells, Texas. She died on 04 Jan 1961 in Waco, Texas. She married JACK C. HARRIS.

    iv. HAZEL LEE WITCHER was born about 1904. She died in 1970 in Cooke County, Texas. She married RALPH COLLINS. She married BILL WEAVER.

7.   v. JO HENRY WITCHER was born on 07 May 1908 in Bells, Texas. She died on 10 Mar 1971 in Denison, Texas. She married KENNETH E. HOOVER.

3. **SAMUEL E.[2] BADGETT** (James Royal[1]) was born on 19 Jun 1878 in Warren County, Kentucky. He died on 31 Aug 1909 in Texas. He married **MARY MAXEY BELOTE**. She was born on 07 Oct 1880 in Grayson County, Texas. She died on 22 May 1963 in Sherman, Texas.

More About Samuel E. Badgett:
Burial: Bells North Cemetery, Bells, Texas
Occupation: 1900 in Bells, Grayson County, Texas; Editor

Notes for Samuel E. Badgett:
Kentucky birth index has June 18, 1878 as date of birth. Headstone has June 19, 1878 as date of birth.

More About Mary Maxey Belote:
Burial: 23 May 1963 in West Hill Cemetery, Grayson County, Texas
Cause Of Death: Auricular Fibrillation and Cardiac Decomposition
Living In: 1910 Living with her son, Clyde, in Collinsville, Grayson County, Texas

Samuel E. Badgett and Mary Maxey Belote had the following child:

    i. CLYDE SAMUEL[3] BADGETT was born on 22 Jan 1904 in Collinsville, Texas. He died on 03 Jun 1976 in Dallas, Texas. He married BEATRICE IMOGENE TURN. She was born on 12 Nov 1910 in San Angelo, Texas. She died on 06 Jun 1995 in Carlsbad, New Mexico.

More About Clyde Samuel Badgett:
Burial: 04 Jun 1976 in Lawnhaven Memorial Gardens, San Angelo, Texas
Occupation: Unit Manager in a Printing Company

4.   **CLAUDE RAY**[2] **BADGETT** (James Royal[1]) was born on 27 Jan 1881 in Kentuckytown, Grayson County, Texas. He died on 18 Apr 1960 in Plainview, Texas. He married Annie Bell Bowie, daughter of Alexander Bowie and Barbara Patterson Bell on 16 Apr 1902 in Coalgate, Choctaw Nation, Indian Territory (Present Day Oklahoma). She was born on 11 Mar 1886 in Krebs, Indian Territory (Present Day Oklahoma). She died on 31 Jan 1978 in Amarillo, Potter County, Texas.

More About Claude Ray Badgett:
Burial: 20 Apr 1960 in Rest Haven Cemetery, Quitaque, Texas
Cause Of Death: Heart Attack
Living In: 1900 Living with his sister, Annie and her family, in Bells, Grayson County, Texas
Living In: 1918 Bells, Texas
Occupation: 1900 in Bells, Grayson County, Texas; Drug Salesman
Occupation: 1910 in Bells, Grayson County, Texas; Druggist in his own Drug Store
Occupation: 1920 in Bells, Grayson County, Texas; Retail Drug Store Owner
Occupation: 1930 in Quitaque, Briscoe County, Texas; Retail Drug Store Merchant
Occupation: 1940 in Quitaque, Briscoe County, Texas; Pharmacist in his own Retail Drugstore

Notes for Claude Ray Badgett:
Owned his own drugstore in Bells, Texas for 28 years. Then owned a drugstore in Quitaque, Texas and later Silverton, Texas.
Lived in Silverton, Texas at the time of his death.

More About Annie Bell Bowie:
Burial: Rest Haven Cemetery, Quitaque, Texas

Notes for Annie Bell Bowie:
Listed in Choctaw Nations Marriage records (Oklahoma).
----
lived in Silverton, Texas at the time of her death.

Headstone has January 30, 1978 for date of death. Death certificate has January 31, 1978 for date of death.

Claude Ray Badgett and Annie Bell Bowie had the following children:

        i.   THYRA[3] BADGETT was born on 09 Feb 1903 in Indian Territory (Present Day Oklahoma). She died on 29 Oct 1967 in Houston, Texas. She married FRANK ASHBURN KING. He was born on 31 Jul 1894 in Texas. He died on 12 Apr 1977 in Dallas County, Texas.

           More About Thyra Badgett:
           Burial: 31 Oct 1967 in Oak Hill Cemetery, Whitewright, Texas
           Cause Of Death: ; Recurrent Cerebral Thrombosis
           Occupation: 1930 in Denison, Grayson County, Texas; Bookkeeper in Bank

8.   ii. MARY BELL BADGETT was born on 19 Oct 1905 in Bells, Texas. She died on 20 Feb 1964 in Houston, Harris County, Texas. She married William Payne Savage, son of

Charles Edward Savage and Flora Belle Payne on 28 Feb 1925 in Grayson County, Texas. He was born on 23 Sep 1903 in Whitewright, Texas. He died in Jul 1970 in Oklahoma City, Oklahoma.

9.   iii. BARBARA ELLEN BADGETT was born on 12 Sep 1912 in Bells, Texas. She died on 03 Nov 2011 in Cockeysville, Maryland. She married Edward Eugene Younger, son of William Randolph Younger and Alma Artelia Rainbolt on 29 Jun 1936 in Quitaque, Texas. He was born on 29 Jun 1909 in Pindall, Arkansas. He died on 23 Jun 1979 in Charlottesville, Virginia.

Generation 3

5. **OPAL**[3] **WITCHER** (Annie Lee[2] Badgett, James Royal[1] Badgett) was born in May 1893 in Texas. She died in 1973 in Grayson County, Texas. She married **CHARLES W. ANDERSON**.

Charles W. Anderson and Opal Witcher had the following child:
      i.   MARY LEE[4] ANDERSON. She married (UNKNOWN) LAMBRE.

6. **FANNIE BELL**[3] **WITCHER** (Annie Lee[2] Badgett, James Royal[1] Badgett) was born on 27 Jan 1897 in Bells, Texas. She died in Oct 1962 in Hobart, Oklahoma. She married William Preston Dugan, son of William Preston Dugan and Lydia Vernon Jones in 1914 in Bells, Texas. He was born on 11 Dec 1893 in Bells, Texas. He died in 1956 in Hobart, Oklahoma.

More About William Preston Dugan:
Living In: 1930 Kiowa County, Oklahoma
Occupation: 1930; Farmer
Occupation: Sheriff of Kiowa County, Oklahoma

William Preston Dugan and Fannie Bell Witcher had the following children:
      i.   MARGARET[4] DUGAN was born about 1921 in Oklahoma.

      ii.   PATRICK DUGAN was born on 30 Jan 1922 in Lone Wolf, Kiowa County, Oklahoma. He died on 18 Jul 1955 in Leoti, Wichita County, Kansas.

          More About Patrick Dugan:
          Burial: Bells North Cemetery, Bells, Texas
          Military Service: U. S. Marine Corps, World War Two and Korea

          Notes for Patrick Dugan:
          Served in U.S. Marine Corps as a fighter pilot, reaching the rank of Major.

      iii. HENRY DUGAN was born about 1926 in Texas.

7. **JO HENRY**[3] **WITCHER** (Annie Lee[2] Badgett, James Royal[1] Badgett) was born on 07 May 1908 in Bells, Texas. She died on 10 Mar 1971 in Denison, Texas. She married **KENNETH E. HOOVER**.

More About Jo Henry Witcher:
Burial: 12 Mar 1971 in Cedarlawn Memorial Park, Sherman, Texas
Cause Of Death: Cardiac Arrest

Kenneth E. Hoover and Jo Henry Witcher had the following child:
10.   i.   KENNETH E[4] HOOVER. He died on 24 Nov 2004. He married (UNKNOWN).

8.   **MARY BELL**[3] **BADGETT** (Claude Ray[2], James Royal[1]) was born on 19 Oct 1905 in Bells, Texas. She died on 20 Feb 1964 in Houston, Harris County, Texas. She married William Payne Savage, son of Charles Edward Savage and Flora Belle Payne on 28 Feb 1925 in Grayson County, Texas. He was born on 23 Sep 1903 in Whitewright, Texas. He died in Jul 1970 in Oklahoma City, Oklahoma.

More About Mary Bell Badgett:
Burial: 25 Feb 1964 in Rest Haven Cemetery, Quitaque, Texas
Cause Of Death: Carcinoma of the Tongue.
Occupation: Worked for Department of State in Washington D, C.

Notes for Mary Bell Badgett:
Head stone has October 19, 1905 as birth date. Headstone has January 20, 1964 for death date which is not correct. Death certificate has October 19, 1904 as birth date and February 20, 1964 as death date. Born Mary Bell Badgett but known as Maribel for most of her life. Her headstone has Maribel on it.

More About William Payne Savage:
Occupation: 1930 in Amarillo, Texas; Bookkeeper in Wholesale Hardware
Occupation: 1940 in Oklahoma City, Oklahoma; Traveling Salesman for Wholesale Hardware
Occupation: Salesman
Military Service: World War Two - U.S. Army - Captain

Notes for William Payne Savage:
Foiund dead in his hotel room in Oklahoma City, Oklahoma. Exact date of death is not certain.

William Payne Savage and Mary Bell Badgett had the following children:

11.   i.   MARIBEL[4] SAVAGE was born on 22 Jun 1926 in Sherman Texas. She died on 14 Feb 2010 in Tampa, Florida. She married ROY GARLAND EDWARDS. He was born on 30 May 1922 in Loraine, Texas. He died on 14 Oct 1974 in Tampa, Florida.

      ii.   CLAUDE RAY SAVAGE was born on 02 Jul 1933 in Briscoe County, Texas. He died on 17 Apr 1984 in Tarrant County, Texas.

            More About Claude Ray Savage:
            Burial: Moore Memorial Gardens, Arlington, Texas
            Living In: 1940 Living with his Badgett grandparents in Quitaque, Briscoe County, Texas.
            Military Service: U. S. Army

9.   **BARBARA ELLEN**[3] **BADGETT** (Claude Ray[2], James Royal[1]) was born on 12 Sep 1912 in Bells, Texas. She died on 03 Nov 2011 in Cockeysville, Maryland. She married Edward Eugene Younger, son of William Randolph Younger and Alma Artelia Rainbolt on 29 Jun 1936 in Quitaque, Texas. He was born on 29 Jun 1909 in Pindall, Arkansas. He died on 23 Jun 1979 in Charlottesville, Virginia.

More About Barbara Ellen Badgett:
Burial: 13 Jul 2013 in University of Virginia Cemetery, Charlottesville, Virginia
Living In: 05 Apr 1930 With her parents in Quitique, Texas
Living In: 23 Apr 1930 As a lodger in Oklahoma City, Oklahoma
Occupation: 1940 in Washington, D.C.; Steno-Typist

Notes for Barbara Ellen Badgett:
Barbara Badgett Younger

Barbara Badgett Younger, 99, of Charlottesville, died on Thursday, November 3, 2011, at Broadmead in Cockeysville, Maryland.

She was born on September 11, 1912, in Bells, Texas. She was preceded in death by her husband of 49 years, Mr. Edward Younger, professor of history at the University of Virginia.

She attended schools in Bells, Texas, and El Reno, Oklahoma, and was president of her freshman class and vice-president of her sophomore class. After her junior year, she entered Oklahoma City University in 1929, where she was a member of Beta Alpha Phi sorority. She then attended West Texas State Teacher's College in Canyon, Texas, receiving a teaching certificate. As a young woman she was well known for her talent and beauty, and she was crowned Queen of the Red River Valley Fair in Paris, Texas and Queen of the "Court of America Beyond the Horizon" at the Plainview, Texas, Dairy Pageant. She began her teaching career on West Texas ranch schools, in one-room schoolhouses where the students rode to school on horseback. In 1936, she married Edward Younger, also a teacher, and 1933 graduate of Arkansas State Teachers College. Mr. Younger then began graduate study at Oklahoma State University and Mrs. Younger worked as office assistant to University president Henry G. Bennett, who was later appointed by President Truman as an Assistant Secretary of State, heading up the Point Four Program that later became USAID. The couple then moved to Washington, D.C., where Mr. Younger completed his Ph.D. in History in 1942.

There Mrs. Younger was a secretary to the Commissioner of the United States Office of Civilian Defense until she "retired" to help her husband with research and type his dissertation. During World War II, Mr. Younger joined the United States Navy and the couple lived in Florida, California, Rhode Island and finally Annapolis, Maryland. In 1946, Mr. Younger joined the faculty of the University of Virginia. He became chair of the History Department in 1962 and was appointed Dean of the Graduate School of Arts and Sciences in 1966. From 1955 until 1979, Barbara and Ed lived on the Grounds; from 1955 until 1967 at 4 Dawson's Row, and from 1967 until 1979 in Pavilion X. From 1957 until 1958, they travelled to live in India where Mr. Younger was Fulbright professor of American history at the University of Allahabad. From 1960 until 1961, they lived in Newport, RI, where Mr. Younger taught maritime history at the Naval War College. Barbara was his partner in all his endeavors for some forty years, opening her home to gatherings of students, faculty, and visiting scholars. She was active in community and University affairs: American Association of University Women, Westminster Presbyterian Church, Faculty Wives Club, where she was President from 1956 until 1957.

After the death of Mr. Younger in 1979, she helped to supervise the completion and publishing of his final book,"The Governors of Virginia Since 1860". She continued to live in Charlottesville and enjoyed an active life of entertaining and international travel until 2005, when she moved to Maryland to live nearer her family. She especially enjoyed time spent with her grandson.

Surviving are Ellen Stromdahl, daughter, Mark Stromdahl, son-in-law, and Larson Stromdahl, grandson.

A private memorial service will be held at Broadmead Retirement Community in Cockeysville, Maryland, on Thursday, November 17, 2011. Interment will be held at the University of Virginia Cemetery at a later date.

Memorial contributions can be made to the Edward and Barbara Younger Award, Corcoran Department of History, University of Virginia. Pay to the order of the College Foundation, P.O. Box 400801, Charlottesville, Virginia, 22904

Published in the Daily Progress on November 10, 2011

    YOUNGER, Barbara, 99, of Charlottesville, died November 3, 2011. She was preceded in death by her husband of 49 years, Edward Younger, professor of history, University of Virginia. She received her teaching certificate at West Texas State Teacher's College and married Mr. Younger in 1936. In 1946, Mr. Younger joined the faculty of the University of Virginia, where he became chair of the History Department in 1962 and was appointed Dean of the Graduate School of Arts and Sciences in 1966. From 1955-1979, the couple lived on the University of Virginia Grounds. In 1957-58, they traveled to live in India, where Mr. Younger was Fulbright professor of University of Allahabad. In 1960-61, they lived in Newport, R.I., where Mr. Younger taught at the Naval War College. Mrs. Younger was his partner in all his endeavors for some 40 years, opening her home to gatherings of students, faculty, and visiting scholars. She was active in community and University affairs. After Mr. Younger's death in 1979, she helped to supervise the completion of his final book, "The Governors of Virginia, 1860 to 1978." She continued to live in Charlottesville until 2005, when she moved to Maryland. Surviving are Ellen Stromdahl, daughter; Mark Stromdahl, son in law; and Larson Stromdahl; grandson. A private memorial service will be held at Broadmead Retirement Community, Cockeysville, Md. on November 17. Interment will be in the University of Virginia Cemetery at a later date. Memorial contributions can be made to the Edward and Barbara Younger Award, Corcoran Department of History, University of Virginia.

Published in Richmond Times-Dispatch on November 10, 2011

Barbara Badgett Younger of Charlottesville passed away on 3 Nov. 2011, at the Broadmead Retirement Community in Cockeysville, MD, and a private memorial service of her life was held there. On Saturday, 13 July, 2013, her remains will be returned to Charlottesville and interred in the University of Virginia Cemetery. She was born on September 11, 1912, in Bells, Texas. She was preceded in death by her husband of 49 years, Mr. Edward Younger, professor of history at the University of Virginia.
She attended schools in Bells, Texas, and El Reno, Oklahoma, and was president of her freshman class and vice-president of her sophomore class. After her junior year, she entered Oklahoma City University in 1929, where she was a member of Beta Alpha Phi sorority. She then attended West Texas State Teacher's College in Canyon, Texas, receiving a teaching certificate. As a young woman she was well known for her talent and beauty, and she was crowned Queen of the Red River Valley Fair in Paris, Texas and Queen of the "Court of America Beyond the Horizon" at the Plainview, Texas, Dairy Pageant. She began her teaching career on West Texas ranch schools, in one-room schoolhouses where the students rode to school on horseback. In 1936, she married Edward Younger, also a teacher, and 1933 graduate of Arkansas State Teachers College. Mr. Younger then began graduate study at Oklahoma State University and Mrs. Younger worked as office assistant to University president Henry G. Bennett, who was later appointed by President Truman as an Assistant Secretary of State, heading up the Point Four Program that later became USAID. The couple then moved to Washington, D.C., where Mr. Younger completed his Ph.D. in History in 1942. There Mrs. Younger was a secretary to the Commissioner of the United States Office of Civilian Defense until she "retired" to help her husband with research and type his dissertation. During World War II, Mr. Younger joined the United States Navy and the couple lived in Florida, California, Rhode Island and finally Annapolis, Maryland. In 1946, Mr. Younger joined the faculty of the University of Virginia. He became chair of the History Department in 1962 and was appointed Dean of the Graduate School of Arts and Sciences in 1966. From 1955 until 1979, Barbara and Ed lived on the Grounds; from 1955 until 1967 at 4 Dawson's Row, and from 1967 until 1979 in Pavilion X. From 1957 until 1958, they travelled to live in India where Mr. Younger was Fulbright professor of American history at the University of Allahabad. From 1960 until 1961, they lived in Newport, RI, where Mr. Younger taught maritime history at the Naval War College. Barbara was his partner in all his endeavors for some forty years, opening her home to gatherings of students, faculty, and visiting scholars. She was active in community and University affairs: American Association of University Women, Westminster Presbyterian Church, Faculty Wives Club, where she was President from 1956 until 1957.
After the death of Mr. Younger in 1979, she helped to supervise the completion and publishing of

his final book, "The Governors of Virginia, 1860-1978". She continued to live in Charlottesville and enjoyed an active life of entertaining and international travel until 2005, when she moved to Maryland to live nearer her family. She especially enjoyed time spent with her grandson. Surviving are Ellen Stromdahl, daughter, Mark Stromdahl, son-in-law, and Larson Stromdahl, grandson.

A graveside service will be held at the University of Virginia Cemetery at 11:00 am, Saturday, 13 July, 2013.

Teague Funeral Services, Charlottesville, Virginia

More About Edward Eugene Younger:
Burial: University of Virginia Cemetery, Charlottesville, Virginia
Living In: Bet. 1910-1930 Prairie Township, Searcy County, Arkansas
Living In: 17 Apr 1930 With his parents in Prarie Township. Searcy County, Arkansas.
Living In: 23 Apr 1930 in As a boarder while he was a school student in Cypress Ridge, Monroe County, Arkansas.
Living In: 1940 Washington, District of Columbia
Occupation: Bet. 1928-1937; Teacher, Principal and Superintendant in Public Schools of Arkansas and Oklahoma
Occupation: Bet. 1937-1938; Teaching Fellow at Oklahoma State University
Occupation: Bet. 1938-194 ; Teaching Fellow at George Washington University
Occupation: Bet. 1945-1946; Instructor of History, U. S. Naval Academy
Occupation: Bet. 1946-1961; Professor of American History, University of Virginia
Military Service: Bet. 17 Aug 1942-May 1954; U.S. Navy, World War 2 (Lt. Commander)

Notes for Edward Eugene Younger:
Head of History Department at the University of Virginia, Charlottesville, Virginia.

Edward Eugene Younger and Barbara Ellen Badgett had the following child:

12.   i. ELLEN BADGETT[4] YOUNGER was born on 05 Sep 1947 in Charlottesville, Virginia. She married (1) JAMES OTIS MOORE, son of James O. Moore on 11 Jan 1966. He was born about 1945. She married MARK STROMDAHL.

Generation 4

10.   **KENNETH E[4] HOOVER** (Jo Henry[3] Witcher, Annie Lee[2] Badgett, James Royal[1] Badgett, Kenneth E.). He died on 24 Nov 2004. He married **(UNKNOWN)**.

Kenneth E Hoover and (Unknown) had the following child:
        i.   DAVID ALLEN[5] HOOVER.

11.   **MARIBEL[4] SAVAGE** (Mary Bell[3] Badgett, Claude Ray[2] Badgett, James Royal[1] Badgett) was born on 22 Jun 1926 in Sherman Texas. She died on 14 Feb 2010 in Tampa, Florida. She married **ROY GARLAND EDWARDS**. He was born on 30 May 1922 in Loraine, Texas. He died on 14 Oct 1974 in Tampa, Florida.

More About Maribel Savage:
Burial: 18 Feb 2010 in Pleasant Grove Cemetery, Durant, Florida
Living In: 1940 Living with her Badgett grandparents in Quitaque, Briscoe County, Texas.

Notes for Maribel Savage:
Born Mary Bell Savage but known as Maribel most of her life. Original birth certificate does not have a first name and amended birth certicate, filed June 20, 1952, has Maribel for her first name.

1940 U.S. Census has her name as Mary Bell Savage.

More About Roy Garland Edwards:
Burial: Pleasant Grove Cemetery, Durant, Florida
Military Service: Bet. 1942-1964; U. S. Air Force (retired as a Major)

Roy Garland Edwards and Maribel Savage had the following children:
13.   i. DAVID GARLAND[5] EDWARDS was born on 21 May 1945 in Fort Sumner, New Mexico. He married Hope Ellen Stewart on 09 Mar 1968 in Tampa, Florida. She was born on 27 Jun 1949 in South Perry, Ohio.

       ii. ROBERT MARION EDWARDS was born on 11 Dec 1946 in Lubbock, Texas.

12. **ELLEN BADGETT[4] YOUNGER** (Barbara Ellen[3] Badgett, Claude Ray[2] Badgett, James Royal[1] Badgett) was born on 05 Sep 1947 in Charlottesville, Virginia. She married (1) **JAMES OTIS MOORE**, son of James O. Moore on 11 Jan 1966. He was born about 1945. She married **MARK STROMDAHL**.

Mark Stromdahl and Ellen Badgett Younger had the following child:
      i. LARSON[5] STROMDAHL.

Generation 5

13. **DAVID GARLAND[5] EDWARDS** (Maribel[4] Savage, Mary Bell[3] Badgett, Claude Ray[2] Badgett, James Royal[1] Badgett) was born on 21 May 1945 in Fort Sumner, New Mexico. He married Hope Ellen Stewart on 09 Mar 1968 in Tampa, Florida. She was born on 27 Jun 1949 in South Perry, Ohio.

More About David Garland Edwards:
Military Service: Bet. Nov 1965-Nov 1967; U. S. Army

David Garland Edwards and Hope Ellen Stewart had the following children:
14.   i. DIANA GAIL[6] EDWARDS was born on 28 Mar 1969 in Plant City, Florida. She married Mark Gregory Simmons on 23 Dec 1988 in Plant City, Florida.

15.   ii. DARLENE MARIE EDWARDS was born on 28 Dec 1970 in Plant City, Florida. She married Randall Edward Thompson on 12 Sep 1993 in Pickerington, Ohio.

     iii. PATRICIA ANNE EDWARDS was born on 20 Oct 1972 in Plant City, Florida. She died on 20 Oct 1972 in Plant City, Florida.

Generation 6

14. **DIANA GAIL[6] EDWARDS** (David Garland[5], Maribel[4] Savage, Mary Bell[3] Badgett, Claude Ray[2] Badgett, James Royal[1] Badgett) was born on 28 Mar 1969 in Plant City, Florida. She married Mark Gregory Simmons on 23 Dec 1988 in Plant City, Florida.

Mark Gregory Simmons and Diana Gail Edwards had the following children:
      i. MARK GREGORY[7] EDWARDS was born on 20 Jun 1988 in Plant City, Florida. He married Julie Ann Mercer on 17 Feb 2007 in Wellston, Ohio. She was born on 28 May 1988.

17.   ii. DAVIAN GAIL SIMMONS was born on 12 Feb 1991 in Monroe, North Carolina. She married JERROD RODGERS.

15. **DARLENE MARIE[6] EDWARDS** (David Garland[5], Maribel[4] Savage, Mary Bell[3] Badgett, Claude Ray[2]

Badgett, James Royal[1] Badgett) was born on 28 Dec 1970 in Plant City, Florida. She married Randall Edward Thompson on 12 Sep 1993 in Pickerington, Ohio.

Randall Edward Thompson and Darlene Marie Edwards had the following children:
- i.   TREVOR[7] THOMPSON was born on 11 Sep 1995.

- ii.   VICTORIA KATHLEEN THOMPSON was born in May 1997.

Generation 7

16.   **DAVIAN GAIL[7] SIMMONS** (Diana Gail[6] Edwards, David Garland[5] Edwards, Maribel[4] Savage, Mary Bell[3] Badgett, Claude Ray[2] Badgett, James Royal[1] Badgett) was born on 12 Feb 1991 in Monroe, North Carolina. She married **JERROD RODGERS**.

Jerrod Rodgers and Davian Gail Simmons had the following child:
- i.   DAVID[8] RODGERS.

NOTES:

DESCENDANTS

OF

EDWARD WARREN GARLAND

Descendants of Edward Warren Garland

Generation 1

1. **EDWARD WARREN**[1] **GARLAND** was born on 28 Oct 1825 in Giles County, Tennessee. He died on 12 May 1897 in Texas. He married (1) **JULIA REBECCA KIMBELL**, daughter of John M. Kimbell and Sarah Angelina Elliott before 1878. She was born on 31 Mar 1845 in Republic of Texas. She died on 26 Jan 1908 in Texas. He married (2) **MARY EMELINE JENKINS**, daughter of James Wilson Jenkins and Sarah Dowd on 18 Jun 1845 in Tishomingo County, Mississippi. She was born on 25 Oct 1827 in Chatham County, North Carolina. She died on 21 Feb 1887 in Hardin County, Tennessee.

More About Edward Warren Garland:
Burial: Garland Cemetery, Red River County, Texas
Living In: 1845 With his uncle, Peter Garland, in Tishomingo County, Mississippi, two doors away from the home of Mary Emeline Jenkins
Living In: Feb 1868 Red River County, Texas
Occupation: 1850 in Tishomingo County, Mississippi; Merchant
Occupation: 1880 in Precinct 7, Red River County, Texas; Farmer
Military Service: Bet. 13 Sep 1847-10 Jul 1848 in Mexican War; Company C, Second Mississippi Infantry, U.S. Army
Military Service: Civil War for C.S.A.
Property: 1869 in Bowie County, Texas; 300 Acres
Property: 1870 in Bowie County, Texas; 300 Acres
Property:1880 in Red River County, Texas; 36 Acres Improved and 50 Acres Unimproved
Property: 1888 in Bowie County, Texas; 108 Acres and 8 city lots in DeKalb
Property: 1889 in Bowie County, Texas; 108 Acres and 8 city lots in DeKalb
Property: 1896 in Bowie County, Texas; 110 Acres and 7 city lots in DeKalb
Property: 1897 in Bowie County, Texas; 110 Acres and 7 city lots in DeKalb

Notes for Edward Warren Garland:
Mustered in for Mexican War at Farmington, Mississippi. Mustered out in Vicksburg, Mississippi.

November 25, 1869 Red River County, Texas voter registration shows Edward having lived in Red River County and Texas 22 months at that time.

More About Julia Rebecca Kimbell:
Burial: Garland Cemetery, Red River County, Texas
Cause Of Death: Infection from a rat bite to her hand while reaching into a corn bin in her barn
Living In: 1900 With her Garland children in Commissioner Precinct 3, Bowie County, Texas
Occupation: 1860 in DeKalb, Texas; Seamstress
Property: 1886 in Bowie County, Texas; 18 Acres

Edward Warren Garland and Julia Rebecca Kimbell had the following children:

> i. JOSEPH EDWARD[2] GARLAND was born on 17 Mar 1878 in Red River County, Texas. He died on 01 Sep 1946 in Lamesa, Dawson County, Texas. He married Lou Ethel Bynum, daughter of Alfred Baker Bynum and Dorinda Sandal Baird on 21 May 1908 in Brownfield, Texas. She was born on 25 Apr 1890 in Whitewright, Grayson County, Texas. She died on 17 Sep 1969 in Lamesa, Dawson County, Texas.

> ii. EMMA GEORGIE IRENE GARLAND was born on 23 Mar 1880 in Annona, Texas. She died on 17 Dec 1969 in Kerrville, Texas. She married LeRoy Ardis Edwards in May 1921 in Roscoe, Texas. He was born on 27 Feb 1881 in Sulphur Springs, Texas. He died on 05 Dec 1951 in Loraine, Texas.

> RUFUS SMIZER MCKINNEY GARLAND was born on 03 Sep 1882 in Texas. He died on

07 Feb 1919 in North Atlantic Ocean (Returning from France after World War One).

More About Rufus Smizer McKinney Garland:
Burial: Loraine, Texas
Cause Of Death: Spanish Flu
Occupation: 1910 Roscoe, Texas; Drug Store Prescriptionist
Occupation: 1917 Loraine, Texas; Pharmacist
Military Service: 1918 in France; World War One (Medic)
Military Service: Spanish American War

Notes for Rufus Smizer McKinney Garland:
Died at sea from flu on the way home from World War One military service in France
Never Married.

4.	iv. MAGGIE AUGUSTA ESTELLE GARLAND was born in Aug 1884 in DeKalb, Texas. She died on 29 Jan 1955 in Sweetwater, Texas. She married Barna Haney, son of William Daniel Haney and Mamie H. Harkins on 24 May 1911 in Roscoe, Texas. He was born on 30 Nov 1887 in Temple, Bell County, Texas. He died on 27 Jan 1957 in Roscoe, Texas.

More About Mary Emeline Jenkins:
Burial: Roberts Cemetery, Conce, Hardin County, Tennessee
Cause Of Death: Consumption

More About Edward Warren Garland and Mary Emeline Jenkins:
Marriage Fact: 16 Jun 1845 in Date of Marriage Bond
Marriage Fact: Ceremony performed by J. C. Lowery, J.P.
Marriage Fact: Garland Family Oral History; Marriage lasted only one day.
Marriage Fact: Surety: G. L. Goff

Generation 2

2.	**JOSEPH EDWARD**[2] **GARLAND** (Edward Warren[1]) was born on 17 Mar 1878 in Red River County, Texas. He died on 01 Sep 1946 in Lamesa, Dawson County, Texas. He married Lou Ethel Bynum, daughter of Alfred Baker Bynum and Dorinda Sandal Baird on 21 May 1908 in Brownfield, Texas. She was born on 25 Apr 1890 in Whitewright, Grayson County, Texas. She died on 17 Sep 1969 in Lamesa, Dawson County, Texas.

More About Joseph Edward Garland:
Burial: 03 Sep 1946 in Lamesa Cemetery, Lamesa, Texas
Cause Of Death: Cerebral Hemorrhage
Living In: 1900 With his mother and siblings in Bowie County, Texas
Occupation: 1900 in Commisioner Precinct 3, Bowie County, Texas; Day Laborer
Occupation: 1910 in Dawson County, Texas; Lawyer
Occupation: 1918 in Lamesa, Texas; County Judge and Attorney
Occupation: 1920 in Lamesa, Texas; Attorney at Law
Occupation: 1930 in Lamesa, Texas; Independant Lawyer
Occupation: 1940 in Lamesa, Texas; Attorney at Law
Military Service: Spanish American War

More About Lou Ethel Bynum:
Burial: 19 Sep 1969 in Lamesa Cemetery, Lamesa, Texas

Cause Of Death: Heart Disease

Joseph Edward Garland and Lou Ethel Bynum had the following children:

      i. EDWARD BYNUM[3] GARLAND was born on 15 Jun 1909 in Texas. He died on 30 Oct 1986 in Seminole, Texas.

        More About Edward Bynum Garland:
        Burial: Lamesa Cemetery, Lamesa, Texas
        Living In: 1930 Living with his parents in Lamesa, Texas
        Living In: 1940 Living with his parents in Lamesa, Texas
        Occupation: 1940 in Lamesa, Dawson County, Texas; Stock Farmer
        Military Service: Bet. 05 Sep 1942-15 Nov 1945; U.S. Army, World War Two

5.   ii. MARGARET DORINDA GARLAND was born on 01 Oct 1911 in Lamesa, Dawson County, Texas. She died on 29 Apr 2005 in Lubbock, Texas. She married James Mack Noble, son of James Mack Noble and Rosia Lee Carter on 01 Jan 1933 in Lamesa, Texas. He was born on 29 Jun 1898 in Texas. He died on 07 Sep 1961 in O'Donnell, Texas.

6.   iii. JAMES GARLAND was born on 20 Sep 1918 in Lamesa, Dawson County, Texas. He died on 25 Feb 1988 in Hobbs, New Mexico. He married (1) EVA MAE WATERS on 01 Jun 1950 in Dawson County, Texas. She was born about 1924. He married DOROTHY (UNKNOWN).

3.   **EMMA GEORGIE IRENE[2] GARLAND** (Edward Warren[1]) was born on 23 Mar 1880 in Annona, Texas. She died on 17 Dec 1969 in Kerrville, Texas. She married LeRoy Ardis Edwards in May 1921 in Roscoe, Texas. He was born on 27 Feb 1881 in Sulphur Springs, Texas. He died on 05 Dec 1951 in Loraine, Texas.

More About Emma Georgie Irene Garland:
Burial: 20 Dec 1969 in Loraine Cemetery,Loraine, Texas
Cause Of Death: Broncho Pneumonia and Arteriosclerosis
Living In: 1920 Lamesa, Texas with sister Estelle and family.
Occupation: 1920 in Lamesa, Texas; Teacher

More About LeRoy Ardis Edwards:
Burial: 07 Dec 1951 in Loraine Cemetery, Loraine, Texas
Cause Of Death: Carcinoma of Lung
Occupation: 1930 in Loraine, Texas; Lumber Yard Manager
Occupation: 1940 in Olton, Texas; Retail Lumber Yard Manager

Notes for LeRoy Ardis Edwards:
Discovered and owned, with his brother Walter, "Baking Powder" gold mine in New Mexico.

LeRoy Ardis Edwards and Emma Georgie Irene Garland had the following child:

7.   i.   ROY GARLAND[3] EDWARDS was born on 30 May 1922 in Loraine, Texas. He died on 14 Oct 1974 in Tampa, Florida. He married Maribel Savage on 08 Apr 1944 in Lubbock, Texas. She was born on 22 Jun 1926 in Sherman, texas. She died on 14 Feb 2010 in Tampa, Florida.

4.   **MAGGIE AUGUSTA ESTELLE[2] GARLAND** (Edward Warren[1]) was born in Aug 1884 in DeKalb, Texas. She died on 29 Jan 1955 in Sweetwater, Texas. She married Barna Haney, son of William Daniel Haney and Mamie H. Harkins on 24 May 1911 in Roscoe, Texas. He was born on 30 Nov 1887 in

Temple, Bell County, Texas. He died on 27 Jan 1957 in Roscoe, Texas.

More About Maggie Augusta Estelle Garland:
Burial: 31 Jan 1955 in Roscoe Cemetery, Roscoe, Texas
Cause Of Death: Cerebral Hemorrhage
Living In: 1910 Living with her brother, Rufus Garland, in Roscoe, Texas
Living In: 1920 Lamesa, Texas
Living In: 1930 Roscoe, Texas
Living In: 1955 Roscoe, Texas
Occupation: 1910 in Roscoe, Texas; Dry Goods Saleslady

More About Barna Haney:
Burial: 28 Jan 1957 in Roscoe Cemetery, Roscoe, Texas
Living In: 1900 Bell County, Texas
Living In: 1910 Living with his parents in Roscoe, Texas
Occupation: 1910 in Roscoe, Texas; Furniture Sales Clerk
Occupation: 1920 in Lamesa, Texas; Clerk in Meyers Drug Company
Occupation: 1930 in Roscoe, Texas; Druggist in Drug Store
Occupation: 1932 in Roscoe, Texas; President of Board of Education
Occupation: 1940 in Roscoe, Texas; Pharmacist and Drug Store owner, Roscoe, Texas

Notes for Barna Haney:
Owned Haney Drug Store, Roscoe, Texas. Mayor and School Board Member of Roscoe, Texas.

More About Barna Haney and Maggie Augusta Estelle Garland:
Marriage License: 23 May 1911 in Nolan County, Texas
Marriage Fact: Married by Rev. J. W. Smith, M. E. Church South, Roscoe, Texas.

Barna Haney and Maggie Augusta Estelle Garland had the following children:

8.	i. WILLIAM GARLAND[3] HANEY was born on 11 May 1912 in Roscoe, Texas. He died on 19 Jan 1988 in Lubbock, Texas. He married Allie Pearl Dunn, daughter of Yanks Dunn and Ada Branson on 04 Oct 1942 in Roscoe, Texas. She was born on 07 Oct 1922 in Burleson, Texas. She died on 29 Apr 2007 in Roscoe, Texas.

9.	ii. MARY JULIA HANEY was born on 16 Aug 1916. She died on 25 Jun 1996 in Clarkesville, Texas. She married Joseph Dellinger Garland, son of Wirt Robert Garland and Lola Prudence Dellinger on 21 Jun 1942 in Roscoe, Texas. He was born on 07 Dec 1914 in Annona, Texas. He died on 16 Aug 1973 in Clarkesville, Texas.

Generation 3

5.	**MARGARET DORINDA[3] GARLAND** (Joseph Edward[2], Edward Warren[1]) was born on 01 Oct 1911 in Lamesa, Dawson County, Texas. She died on 29 Apr 2005 in Lubbock, Texas. She married James Mack Noble, son of James Mack Noble and Rosia Lee Carter on 01 Jan 1933 in Lamesa, Texas. He was born on 29 Jun 1898 in Texas. He died on 07 Sep 1961 in O'Donnell, Texas.

More About Margaret Dorinda Garland:
Burial: 03 May 2005 in O'Donnell Cemetery, O'Donnell, Texas

Notes for Margaret Dorinda Garland:
Lubbock Avalanche-Journal

Obituary of Margaret Garland Noble
Published: Monday, May 02, 2005

Margaret Garland Noble, 93, of Lubbock and formerly of ODonnell died Friday, April 29, 2005 at Grace House in Lubbock. She was born Sept. 30, 1911 in Lamesa. She married James Mack Noble, Jr. Jan. 1, 1933 in Lamesa. He preceded her in death in 1961.

Mrs. Noble was the daughter of Joseph Edward and Ethel Garland, who were early pioneer settlers in Dawson and Lynn counties. She was a world traveler, seeing places like China, Australia, New Zealand and Central America. In 1981, she and her family traveled to Scandanavia and Russia.

Margaret was employed by the U.S. Postal Service as a mail carrier. She belonged to Tuesday Bridge and Study Club in ODonnell.

Two brothers, James and Edward, also precede her in death.

Survivors include: two sons, Edward Garland of San Francisco Bay Area, Calif. and James Mack, III of Longview; two grandchildren; and two great-grandchildren.

Services will be 4 p.m. Tuesday at First United Methodist Church in ODonnell with the Rev. Kenneth Peterson officiating.

Burial will be in ODonnell Cemetery.

The family suggests memorial to the ODonnell Cemetery Association or a charity of choice.

Birth date is from birth certificate.

More About James Mack Noble:
Burial: 09 Sep 1961 in O'Donnell Cemetery, O'Donnell, Texas
Cause Of Death: Acute Coronary Thrombosis
Occupation: 1940 in O'Donnell, Texas; Post Master of U.S. Post Office
Occupation: 1961 in O'Donnell, Texas; Mail Carrier
Military Service: World War One

James Mack Noble and Margaret Dorinda Garland had the following children:

10.   i.   JAMES MACK[4] NOBLE was born on 10 Dec 1933 in Dawson County, Texas. He married JESSICA (UNKNOWN).

     ii.   EDWARD GARLAND NOBLE was born on 19 Aug 1936 in Dawson County, Texas.

6.   **JAMES[3] GARLAND** (Joseph Edward[2], Edward Warren[1]) was born on 20 Sep 1918 in Lamesa, Dawson County, Texas. He died on 25 Feb 1988 in Hobbs, New Mexico. He married (1) **EVA MAE WATERS** on 01 Jun 1950 in Dawson County, Texas. She was born about 1924. He married **DOROTHY (UNKNOWN)**.

More About James Garland:
Burial: Dawson County Cemetery, Lamesa, Dawson County, Texas
Occupation: 1940 in Honolulu, Hawaii Territory; Medical Department, Tripler General Hospital, U.S. Army
Military Service: Bet. 1940-1945; World War Two

Notes for James Garland:
Present during Japanese attack on Pearl Harbor, December 7, 1941.

Served in Europe- Normandy to V.E. Day.
Divorced from Eva Waters on January 16, 1974 in Gaines County, Texas.

James Garland and Eva Mae Waters had the following children:
xi.   i. MARGARET LOU[4] GARLAND. She married MIKE RYAN. ii.

JAMES GARLAND.

7.   **ROY GARLAND**[3] **EDWARDS** (Emma Georgie Irene[2] Garland, Edward Warren[1] Garland) was born on May 1922 in Loraine, Texas. He died on 14 Oct 1974 in Tampa, Florida. He married Maribel Savage on 08 Apr 1944 in Lubbock, Texas. She was born on 22 Jun 1926 in Sherman, texas. She died on 14 Feb 2010 in Tampa, Florida.

More About Roy Garland Edwards:
Burial: Pleasant Grove Cemetery, Durant, Florida
Cause Of Death: Heart Failure
Military Service: Bet. 1942-1964; U.S. Air Force (Major)

More About Maribel Savage:
Burial: Pleasant Grove Cemetery, Durant, Florida
Military Service: Bet. 1942-1964

Roy Garland Edwards and Maribel Savage had the following children:
12.   i. DAVID GARLAND[4] EDWARDS was born on 21 May 1945 in Fort Sumner, New Mexico. He married Hope Ellen Stewart on 09 Mar 1968 in Tampa, Florida. She was born on 27 Jun 1949 in South Perry, Ohio.

     ii.   ROBERT MARION EDWARDS was born on 11 Dec 1946 in Lubbock, Texas. He died on 13 Feb 2010 in San Francisco, California.

8.   **WILLIAM GARLAND**[3] **HANEY** (Maggie Augusta Estelle[2] Garland, Edward Warren[1] Garland) was born on 11 May 1912 in Roscoe, Texas. He died on 19 Jan 1988 in Lubbock, Texas. He married Allie Pearl Dunn, daughter of Yanks Dunn and Ada Branson on 04 Oct 1942 in Roscoe, Texas. She was born on 07 Oct 1922 in Burleson, Texas. She died on 29 Apr 2007 in Roscoe, Texas.

More About William Garland Haney: Burial:
Roscoe Cemetery, Roscoe, Texas
Living In: 1940 Living with his parents in Roscoe, Texas
Occupation: 1940 in Roscoe, Texas; Retail Drug Clerk
Occupation: Pharmacist
Military Service: Enlisted at Lubbock, Texas, January 15, 1942 in U.S. Army for World War Two

Notes for William Garland Haney: Held
rank of SSgt. while in U.S. Army.

More About Allie Pearl Dunn:
Burial: Roscoe Cemetery, Roscoe, Texas

Notes for Allie Pearl Dunn:
From THE SWEETWATER (TX) REPORTER (4/30/2007): Allie

Pearl Haney

Funeral services for Allie Pearl Haney, 84, of Roscoe will be held at 10 a.m. Tuesday, May 1, 2007, in the First United Methodist Church of Roscoe with Pastor Tony Wofford and the Rev. Vernon Baker officiating.

Burial will follow in the Roscoe Cemetery under the direction of McCoy Funeral Home of Roscoe.

The family will receive friends from 6-8 p.m. Monday, April 30, 2007, in the funeral home.

Mrs. Haney died Sunday, April 29, 2007, in Roscoe.

She was born on Oct. 7, 1922, in Burleson. She married William Garland Haney on Oct. 4, 1942, in Roscoe. Mrs. Haney was a member of the First United Methodist Church of Roscoe, where she taught Sunday school for many, many years. She lived most of her life in Roscoe, where she and her husband owned and operated Haney Drug and Haney Jewelry. She was a graduate of Roscoe High School. Mrs. Haney was a friend to all and is remembered by her family as their "One True Pearl."

Survivors include two daughters, Peggy Sue Parrot and her husband, Henry Don, of Roscoe, and Jackie Hackfeld and her husband, Keith, of Snyder; one son, Bill Haney and his wife, Nita, of Kansas City, Mo.; one sister, Peggy Richburg and her husband, Charles, of Roscoe; one brother, Buster Dunn and his wife, Wanda, of Roscoe; eight grandchildren and nine great-grandchildren.

She was preceded in death by her husband, William Haney, on Jan. 19, 1988.

William Garland Haney and Allie Pearl Dunn had the following children:

13. i. WILLIAM GARLAND[4] HANEY JR. was born on 21 Jun 1944 in Randolph A.F.B., Texas. He married Nita Ann Buckner in Roscoe, Texas. She was born on 15 Jan 1945.

14. ii. PEGGY SUSAN HANEY was born on 29 Jan 1950. She married Henry Don Parrott in Roscoe, Texas. He was born on 05 Nov 1943.

15. iii. JACKIE ANN HANEY was born on 01 Feb 1958 in Sweetwater, Texas. She married Keith Alfred Hackfeld in Roscoe, Texas.

9. **MARY JULIA[3] HANEY** (Maggie Augusta Estelle[2] Garland, Edward Warren[1] Garland) was born on 16 Aug 1916. She died on 25 Jun 1996 in Clarkesville, Texas. She married Joseph Dellinger Garland, son of Wirt Robert Garland and Lola Prudence Dellinger on 21 Jun 1942 in Roscoe, Texas. He was born on 07 Dec 1914 in Annona, Texas. He died on 16 Aug 1973 in Clarkesville, Texas.

More About Mary Julia Haney:
Burial: 29 Jun 1996 in Garland Cemetery, Annona, Texas
Living In: 1940 Living with her parents in Roscoe, Texas.
Occupation: 1940 in Roscoe, Texas; Music Teacher
Occupation: Music Teacher, Pianist, Organist

More About Joseph Dellinger Garland:
b: 07 Dec 1914
Burial: 18 Aug 1973 in Garland Cemetery, Annona, Texas
Cause Of Death: Acute Myocardial Infarction
Occupation: Banker
Occupation: Welfare Agent
Military Service: SSgt., United States army

Joseph Dellinger Garland and Mary Julia Haney had the following children:

16.   i. SYLVIA ESTELLE[4] GARLAND was born on 24 Mar 1945 in Goose Creek, Texas. She married Joseph Theodore Leeds on 24 Nov 1966 in Clarkesville, Texas. He was born on 16 Sep 1942.

        ii. JUDY FRANCES GARLAND was born on 20 Mar 1948 in Roscoe, Texas. She died on 11 Feb 1993 in Dallas, Texas.

        More About Judy Frances Garland:
        Burial: 14 Feb 1993 in Garland Cemetery, Red River County, Texas

17.   iii. LILLIAN ELIZABETH GARLAND was born on 26 Nov 1951. She married Michael J. Lyons on 29 Oct 1982 in Dallas, Texas. He was born on 09 Oct 1942 in Little Rock, Arkansas.

Generation 4

10.   **JAMES MACK[4] NOBLE** (Margaret Dorinda[3] Garland, Joseph Edward[2] Garland, Edward Warren[1] Garland) was born on 10 Dec 1933 in Dawson County, Texas. He married **JESSICA (UNKNOWN)**.

James Mack Noble and Jessica (unknown) had the following children:
        i. JIM[5] NOBLE. He married JENNIFER (UNKNOWN).

        More About Jim Noble:
        Occupation: Federal Prosecutor

19.   ii. CATHERINE NOBLE. She married TODD MILLER.

11.   **MARGARET LOU[4] GARLAND** (James[3], Joseph Edward[2], Edward Warren[1]). She married **MIKE RYAN**.

Mike Ryan and Margaret Lou Garland had the following child:
        i. AMY[5] RYAN.

12.   **DAVID GARLAND[4] EDWARDS** (Roy Garland[3], Emma Georgie Irene[2] Garland, Edward Warren[1] Garland) was born on 21 May 1945 in Fort Sumner, New Mexico. He married Hope Ellen Stewart on 09 Mar 1968 in Tampa, Florida. She was born on 27 Jun 1949 in South Perry, Ohio.

David Garland Edwards and Hope Ellen Stewart had the following children:
19.   i. DIANA GAIL[5] EDWARDS was born on 28 Mar 1969. She married Mark Gregory Simmons on 23 Dec 1988 in Plant City, Florida.

20.   ii. DARLENE MARIE EDWARDS was born on 28 Dec 1970 in Plant City, Florida. She married Randall Edward Thompson on 12 Sep 1993 in Pickerington, Ohio.

        iii. PATRICIA ANNE EDWARDS was born on 20 Oct 1972 in Plant City, Florida. She died on 20 Oct 1972 in Plant City, Florida.

        More About Patricia Anne Edwards:
        Burial: Pleasant Grove Cemetery, Durant, Florida

13.   **WILLIAM GARLAND[4] HANEY JR.** (William Garland[3], Maggie Augusta Estelle[2] Garland, Edward Warren[1] Garland) was born on 21 Jun 1944 in Randolph A.F.B., Texas. He married Nita Ann

Buckner in Roscoe, Texas. She was born on 15 Jan 1945.

William Garland Haney Jr. and Nita Ann Buckner had the following children:

21.   i.   GABRIEL GARLAND[5] HANEY was born on 02 Feb 1974. He married HEATHER LEE (UNKNOWN).

    ii.   CASEY HAMILTON HANEY was born on 12 Dec 1977.

14.   **PEGGY SUSAN[4] HANEY** (William Garland[3], Maggie Augusta Estelle[2] Garland, Edward Warren[1] Garland) was born on 29 Jan 1950. She married Henry Don Parrott in Roscoe, Texas. He was born on 05 Nov 1943.

Henry Don Parrott and Peggy Susan Haney had the following children:

    i.   JAMES HENRY[5] PARROTT was born on 01 Jun 1972.

    ii.   WILLIAM DANIEL PARROTT was born on 06 May 1974.

    iii.   MELISSA GAIL PARROTT was born on 07 Apr 1976.

15.   **JACKIE ANN[4] HANEY** (William Garland[3], Maggie Augusta Estelle[2] Garland, Edward Warren[1] Garland) was born on 01 Feb 1958 in Sweetwater, Texas. She married Keith Alfred Hackfeld in Roscoe, Texas.

Keith Alfred Hackfeld and Jackie Ann Haney had the following children:

    i.   BRANDON KEITH[5] HACKFELD was born on 10 Aug 1979.

    ii.   BRADY HACKFELD was born on 18 Jan 1982.

    iii.   CHELSEA GAYLE HACKFELD was born on 25 Jan 1988.

16.   **SYLVIA ESTELLE[4] GARLAND** (Mary Julia[3] Haney, Maggie Augusta Estelle[2], Edward Warren[1]) was born on 24 Mar 1945 in Goose Creek, Texas. She married Joseph Theodore Leeds on 24 Nov 1966 in Clarkesville, Texas. He was born on 16 Sep 1942.

Joseph Theodore Leeds and Sylvia Estelle Garland had the following children:

    i.   JOSEPH CHRISTOPHER[5] LEEDS was born on 08 Sep 1971 in Dallas, Texas.

23.   ii.   MARY ELIZABETH LEEDS was born on 26 Feb 1977 in Odessa, Texas. She married EDWARD ELTON BEIERSCHMITT. He was born in Indiana.

    iii.   SAMUEL EDWARD LEEDS was born on 21 Feb 1981 in Mesquite, Texas.

17.   **LILLIAN ELIZABETH[4] GARLAND** (Mary Julia[3] Haney, Maggie Augusta Estelle[2], Edward Warren[1]) was born on 26 Nov 1951. She married Michael J. Lyons on 29 Oct 1982 in Dallas, Texas. He was born on 09 Oct 1942 in Little Rock, Arkansas.

Michael J. Lyons and Lillian Elizabeth Garland had the following child:

    i.   MICHAEL P.[5] LYONS was born on 26 Jul 1973 in Hurst, Texas.

Generation 5

18.   **CATHERINE[5] NOBLE** (James Mack[4], Margaret Dorinda[3] Garland, Joseph Edward[2] Garland, Edward Warren[1] Garland, James Mack[4], James Mack, James Mack, Levi, Stephen, William Dukes). She married **TODD MILLER.**

More About Catherine Noble:
Occupation: School Teacher

More About Todd Miller:
Occupation: Optometrist

Todd Miller and Catherine Noble had the following child:
   i.   CAITLIN[6] MILLER.

19.   **DIANA GAIL[5] EDWARDS** (David Garland[4], Roy Garland[3], Emma Georgie Irene[2] Garland, Edward Warren[1] Garland) was born on 28 Mar 1969. She married Mark Gregory Simmons on 23 Dec 1988 in Plant City, Florida.

   Mark Gregory Simmons and Diana Gail Edwards had the following children:
   i.   MARK GREGORY[6] EDWARDS was born on 20 Jun 1988 in Plant City, Florida. He married Julie Ann Mercer on 17 Feb 2007 in Wellston, Ohio. She was born on 28 May 1988.

   ii.   DAVIAN GAIL SIMMONS was born on 12 Feb 1991 in Monroe, North Carolina.

20.   **DARLENE MARIE[5] EDWARDS** (David Garland[4], Roy Garland[3], Emma Georgie Irene[2] Garland, Edward Warren[1] Garland) was born on 28 Dec 1970 in Plant City, Florida. She married Randall Edward Thompson on 12 Sep 1993 in Pickerington, Ohio.

   Randall Edward Thompson and Darlene Marie Edwards had the following children:
   i.   TREVOR[6] THOMPSON was born on 11 Sep 1995.

   ii.   VICTORIA KATHLEEN THOMPSON was born in May 1997.

21.   **GABRIEL GARLAND[5] HANEY** (William Garland[4] Jr., William Garland[3], Maggie Augusta Estelle[2] Garland, Edward Warren[1] Garland) was born on 02 Feb 1974. He married **HEATHER LEE (UNKNOWN)**.

   Gabriel Garland Haney and Heather Lee (unknown) had the following child:
   i.   SAHARA SNOW[6] HANEY.

22.   **MARY ELIZABETH[5] LEEDS** (Sylvia Estelle[4] Garland, Mary Julia[3] Haney, Maggie Augusta Estelle[2] Garland, Edward Warren[1] Garland) was born on 26 Feb 1977 in Odessa, Texas. She married **EDWARD ELTON BEIERSCHMITT**. He was born in Indiana.

   Edward Elton Beierschmitt and Mary Elizabeth Leeds had the following children:
   i.   BRICE COLE[6] BEIERSCHMITT was born on 01 Apr 1999.

   ii.   LINUS LEEDS BEIERSCHMITT was born on 15 Mar 2000.

Mary Bell Badgett

William Bell and Ann Patterson

Emma Georgie Irene Garland